OUR ADOPTION ADVENTURE

A Family's Journey Through Infertility, Adoption, and Raising Adopted Kids

Jane Carter & David Carter

Our Adoption Adventure

First published in the United Kingdom in January 2019
by My Castle Publishing LLP
www.mycastlepublishing.com

This edition published in July 2019
by My Castle Property Training LLP
© 2019 Jane Carter & David Carter

Jane Carter and David Carter have asserted their right to be identified as the authors of this work in accordance with sections 77 and 78 of the Copyright, Designs and Patents Act 1988.

All rights reserved. No part of this book may be reproduced by any means, electronic, mechanical, photocopying or otherwise, without the prior permission of the publisher.

British Library Cataloguing in Publication Data
A catalogue record is available for this book

Paperback ISBN: 9781792965463

Cover Photo by Daiga Ellaby on Unsplash

My Castle Property Training LLP
2 Maids Close, Biddenden, Kent TN27 8HS, United Kingdom.

Contents

Introduction 7

Part One: Jane's Story 9
Chapter One:
The Beginning 9

Chapter Two:
Medical Intervention 11

Chapter Three:
Starting the Adoption Process 15

Chapter Four:
False Start 21

Chapter Five:
Summer 23

Chapter Six:
Christopher 27

Chapter Seven:
Moving Forward 35

Part Two: David's Story 39
Chapter Eight:
My Childhood 39

Chapter Nine:
Is That Semen in Your Pocket? 49

Chapter Ten:
Under a Magnifying Glass 57

Chapter Eleven:
Hope 73

Chapter Twelve:
It's a Boy 79

Part Three: An Interview With Nanna 87
Chapter Thirteen:
What was it like being a parent? 87

Chapter Fourteen:
Your Thoughts on Jane Not Conceiving 91

Chapter Fifteen:
Then You Told Me You Were Going to Adopt 93

Part Four: Our Children's Thoughts 95
Chapter Sixteen:
An Interview with Summer–8 Years Old 95

Chapter Seventeen:
An interview with Christopher–7 Years Old 97

Part Five: 99
Chapter Eighteen:
Conclusion 99

Part Six: 101
Chapter Nineteen:
Our Ten Tips for Adopters 101

Part Seven: 121
Useful Resources 121

We would like to thank our parents for all the support they gave us, and continue to provide. We could not have taken this journey alone.

Thanks to our children who have given us love, purpose, tickles and a big hug every day.

FREE RESOURCES
Visit our website for Free adoption resources:
mycastlepublishing.com/adopt-resources

Our Adoption Adventure

Introduction

"I spent my late teens and most of my twenties trying not to get pregnant. I assumed that once we started trying for a baby, that it would happen immediately (or maybe take a few months). Things didn't exactly go according to plan."

The book you hold is the story of a couple's journey to becoming adoptive parents. I read plenty of those myself in the harrowing few years that we went through the "adoption process." Looking back though—they left us ill-prepared for our actual experience. One thing all the books sorely lacked, was anything from the Dad's perspective.

David and I wrote our parts of this book on our own. I feel that will be invaluable to you, as we seemed to have focused on different parts of our adoption journey. David wrote heavily about the adoption process itself, and the tasks we were required to tick off. I spent more time writing about what happened after we'd adopted our children. There were parts of the puzzle that one of us remembered, and the other forgot. We also learned from each other, as there were some things that we'd done alone, and hadn't talked about—it was interesting to read.

As a family, we are now at a place where we can look back and hopefully give an honest perspective from the inside, from that of a couple, mother, father and from the children. My kids are now seven and eight years old, and are starting to understand more about their history. I have also spoken honestly with my Mum, as she was intimately involved, and is a hands-on "Nana."

My hope is that by reading our story it will give you some insight into what you are signing up to, and what you could expect. Perhaps most importantly, you may resonate with the feelings we experienced over those years…with some amazing highs…and lows. Seek comfort in knowing that you are not alone in experiencing these negative emotions.

Jane Carter

Part One: Jane's Story

CHAPTER ONE:

The Beginning

David and I met when I was 18 and he was 24. I was immediately captivated by his sophistication, and it didn't take long for us to become quite serious. He was actually quite shy, and of the two of us, I was probably the more emotionally mature. He was kind, and I could see us having a long life together. In fact, after six months, I told him I was planning to marry him. He didn't really take me seriously, but we did talk about families. He and I both came from stable married parents with two kids, and that is what we both wanted for ourselves. We had plenty of time.

When I was at university we squashed into the single bed of my dorm and rented a flat together after that. We bought our first house, and the next one two years later. We were happy and loved being a couple. It took me a long time to convince him to marry me (although he agreed in principle—he took six years to get his head around actually pulling the trigger.)

We finally got married when I was 23. We easily remember our anniversary as we went to the States on our honeymoon two months after 9/11 and got "special security treatment" at every airport. They emptied out our entire luggage including underwear, whilst TV channels filmed us.

I was ready to start trying for a family, but again it took David a while to come to terms with the idea. He assumed—as I did, that as soon as we started trying I would get pregnant, and that would be that. He finally agreed when I was 27, and we stopped using the birth control pill. It felt like an exciting time, and we were embarking on a new chapter in our lives…becoming parents rather than a couple.

We became a little more concerned and disappointed each month that I didn't get pregnant. Sex became more routine and timed; I started buying ovulation test kits. I became more aware of pregnant people on the street and more sensitive to people telling everyone they were pregnant—I felt sad, disappointed and jealous. But we were not really worried…yet.

Part One: Jane's Story

CHAPTER TWO:

Medical Intervention

After trying for a year, I made an appointment with David to see my doctor. I was a little overweight, but the Doctor found no obvious reason that I hadn't conceived yet. He referred us to a hospital for further testing. After a bit of a wait, we had a consultation with a doctor I could barely understand, due to his accent. He explained that the next step was a laparoscopy operation to investigate whether I had any gynaecological problems. This didn't sound like much fun. I had never had an operation before, but this was a step I had to take. I realised that I was risking my life now to have children—but the risk seemed worth it. We didn't really investigate or understand what they were looking for—although I am sure he probably explained—I just didn't take it in.

We waited for eight months to get a slot. Due to the extortionate cost of parking at the hospital, David dropped me off and went home…which was a mistake. The operation went fine, but when the surgeon came to talk to me in the recovery room, I was alone. He said that they had found Stage IV Endometriosis. There are four stages—and IV is the worst. If it had been minor they would have removed it during my operation, but as it was extensive, the risk of cutting my bowel and having to do a larger incision was too great. I hadn't heard of Endometriosis at the time, and it was really upsetting to be told that I had a major problem, and that it would really impact my chances of getting pregnant.

Reading up further at home we established that Stage IV people had a really small chance of conceiving naturally, as the womb tissue gums up the whole area, causing scar tissue and organs to stick together in odd positions—it makes getting pregnant difficult and carrying a baby problematic. Going from "we have been trying for a while—it's a bit annoying" to "unlikely to conceive" in one day was devastating.

Fortunately for us, the NHS funded one round of IVF in our county. We had to wait for the best part of a year, but eventually got our first appointment. Due to the Endo, they decided to put me in an artificial menopause for three months, to try to make it inactive. This involved me injecting myself daily in the thigh and stomach with a big needle. I bruise easily, so looked like a punching bag. I became more emotional (!) and had hot sweats every day, not fun.

The IVF really ramps up your hormones, and as things weren't in the right place I had to have another operation to remove the eggs. You get a call to let you know how your eggs are fertilising—mine weren't that great, but they had enough, and I went back in to have two of them inserted. Not under general anaesthetic this time, but painful nonetheless.

And then we waited…Hooray; I was pregnant for the first time…

…temporarily it turned out. Two weeks later we cried together. My parents consoled me.

That was it for the free treatment. We waited again, before having an MRI. Speaking to the specialist afterwards, he kindly but bluntly told us that there wasn't much point in doing another round of IVF, without surgery to remove the Endo first.

We went home and started researching Endo in earnest. From our understanding the surgery was risky (mine went all around my bowel and had a risk of leaving me with a colostomy bag). Although the chance of conceiving wasn't too bad afterwards—scarring caused problems inside and repeat surgery was necessary every few years. IVF also puts quite a toll on the body with the high levels of hormones and stress to the system.

We decided the risks to my health were too great—and started to consider other options. This was a massive decision for us, and I felt like I was a failure as a person. But we still wanted children.

We looked briefly at surrogacy, but it didn't seem like much of an option in the UK. We didn't have a huge pot of money; my sister had yet to have children, and my Mum couldn't do it, so we dismissed it.

The last option was adoption. This was never something we'd considered before. We had always assumed, even when we were doing the IVF, that we would have our own genetic birth children. Adoption seemed like the last resort, but we contacted the local council and put our names down for the two-hour introduction evening.

Part One: Jane's Story

CHAPTER THREE:

Starting the Adoption Process

Looking back we did not really explore any other options regarding adoption agencies. You can choose your local council, another council, or a private adoption agency. We did a little research and it seemed to us that children being removed by a council would be placed "in-house" first—and if they couldn't find a match in their own pool of adopters they would work with other councils or agencies to place them. As we were after younger children who were more in demand, we decided to work with our local council in the first instance—and fortunately, we met their criteria for adopters at the time.

We had not really processed the fact that we were giving up on our birth children. We were just moving onto the next thing. I think in retrospect that I was really depressed at this stage. I found myself sitting and staring, sitting and crying, and feeling really empty inside. It was like someone had died.

Speaking to a counsellor at the hospital after the IVF failure, she told us that we were grieving for our unborn children—that helped me to make sense of my heartbreak. I knew other people who had lost babies to miscarriage, and although we did not have specific children we were grieving for, it was for all of them. Our two birth children we were never going to have. My fertility…my chance to carry a baby and deliver it…to have a tiny baby of my own. We started the adoption process whilst we were still grieving. I am grateful for the emotional help that our social worker gave us to identify our feelings and move on from them.

Our local council were doing a recruitment drive for new adopters at that time— and as we were looking to have siblings, we were met with open arms. We were allocated to a group and attended four two-day sessions over a few months. There were six families (four couples, one single lady with her mum, and a lady on her own). We think back on that time as our "adoption boot camp". We shared incredibly intimate life stories— all different, and most full of heart-breaking emotion. You don't generally decide to go through adoption, without some trauma.

We bonded with them, and most of us still meet up every six months or so—nine years later. We were saturated with saddening stories about the children coming through the system, worst-case scenarios—and they drummed into us to always think about attachment, attachment, attachment. Although we took it all in, we hoped that we would have an easier journey than some of the cases we were looking at. There were tears and chocolate brownies. We all made it through.

Then we had to wait for a social worker to take on our case. We met with her every couple of weeks for a year, whilst she prepared us for the adoption panel. There

Part One: Jane's Story

was a list of topics that we had to work through, both together and individually—talking about our relationship, experiences, hopes, levels of acceptance and countless other things.

Our social worker initially helped us to overcome our grief, acting as a bit of a counsellor, and moved us towards the expectations we needed to parent an adopted child. We did hours and hours of homework. I was thankful that I didn't have a full-time job, as I spent at least one or two days a week either in meetings, or writing out essays, timelines, support network charts, and endless things to satisfy her that we were ready to go to the panel.

Due to the fact that we were the first amongst our friends to have kids, we had very little experience with children. Initially, I got some work experience, and later a part-time job at a nursery.

David volunteered at a Sure Start Centre just to tick the box. We both thought it was overkill at the time…but retrospectively, this was actually amazingly helpful for the logistics of being a parent. We were able to see the range of development at different ages for different children, and at least the practicalities of looking after a baby were not new. The first few months of working at the nursery I was looking after tiny babies, I was mostly concerned about not dropping them—but I got over that fear. I also did a lot of nappies and became a pro with the wrigglers. I got to know another lady who had adopted her niece.

We drank a bottle of wine most nights after a social

worker visit—it felt like going through the wringer emotionally, being "assessed" all the while. She was finally satisfied that we were going to be "good enough" parents. I feel that all adopters have to be SUPER PARENTS—to be "good enough" to cope with the challenges of having an adopted child. "Good enough" might work for children with no additional emotional needs. We have to be SUPER every day, just to get through the day sometimes.

So we had a date for the Adoption Panel. There were about a dozen people in the room who were social workers, managers, and medical staff. There were others who were there because they'd been involved in the adoption process and had different perspectives, such as previous adopters, adult adoptees, and foster carers. It's basically a group of people who can between them discuss you, and your suitability to be a parent. It is harrowing—like the most important job interview of your life. As adoption was really the last chance for us to have children at all—it felt like the most important day of our lives. We were grilled for what seemed like a long time—but was probably about forty minutes. Fortunately, they let us know verbally on the day we had passed. More wine.

For some people, they have children in mind for them immediately—one of our group got their details of their potential children straight away. They felt us out for a pair of boys who were in the system, giving us some of their background information and ages, but not much more than that. We were interested potentially—and excited, but it turned out that the birth family lived too close to us, so they ended up being placed with another

Part One: Jane's Story

family in our boot camp group.

Each stage felt like a mountain to climb—and people had warned us that the next one was the hardest. Deciding to adopt is like an unending pregnancy. When you are actually pregnant you have a due date, and give or take a few weeks you know when you are due to have your child. Once you are "approved to adopt" you're waiting to be matched with a child—but you don't know how many children (for us one or two), the sex, age, or issues you are going to have to deal with down the road. Most of all, you don't know WHEN it will happen.

You are asked to make a Welcome Book with pictures of your home, and prepare their bedroom as much as you can. We couldn't buy a bed as we weren't sure if we'd need a bed or a cot (or two), or both. So you wait...

Then the people around you get pregnant. Close friends are sensitive, as they know you're adopting/infertile/massively emotional about children. Other are not.

I went to a wedding of one of my nursery work friends and a guy spent twenty minutes telling me how his girlfriend (my friend) had just found out she was five months pregnant, and how surprised and excited they were. It was awful for me, but he had no idea of the bundle of emotions I hid behind my smile.

Our Adoption Adventure

Part One: Jane's Story

CHAPTER FOUR:

False Start

Some months later we had a call from our social worker about a little boy. He was eleven months old and they were looking to place him with us. Ten months was generally the youngest age that children were available to adopt at the time, as it took them that long to assess the situation and the family from birth. We were ecstatic. We had the child's forms, and he looked okay. A specialist was assessing him, as they thought he might have cerebral palsy—but it was difficult to tell at that age. We agreed to go ahead despite the risks.

Our county had a policy of a "blind meet and greet". That meant that we could meet the child—before deciding to proceed to panel for them. As he was so young we met the foster parents and had a chat, then met them in the library with the boy for twenty minutes—not mentioning anything in front of him. It seemed to go well and the foster carers seemed fine.

Later we got a call from our social worker saying that the foster carer had fed back that we had said inappropriate things, and touched him (which was not really allowed). We were really upset, as it wasn't how the meeting had gone at all. It turned out that they had been missing medical appointments and had bad mouthed us deliberately, as they intended to sabotage the placement.

They had fostered him for a year and were looking to adopt him. They had obviously fallen in love with him—and were willing to do what it took to adopt him themselves. I felt angry for quite a long time—we were a couple of weeks from having a child, and it was possible that they could have prevented us from adopting at all. Fortunately, our social worker believed us, and although we couldn't proceed with him, we were back on the list again.

Part of the adoption assessment is looking at your attitude to risk with a child—your boundaries as to what you will accept. It's difficult but necessary. We had set boundaries when it was all-academic—ages, sexes, levels of trauma, physical disability, sexual abuse, behaviour problems, etc. However, once we were matched with an actual child we were perhaps too desperate to accept potential disabilities that we'd previously said no to. We were over eager to become parents. It was a very difficult experience, but perhaps things turned out the best for the boy and for us.

By now I was 33 and David 39. Our lives had been on hold since we started trying to get pregnant four years previously. We couldn't extend or move house, jobs, gain weight, or do anything that would change our circumstances for all that time. We read every adoption book we could find and did all the post-panel training courses. We were in limbo.

Part One: Jane's Story

CHAPTER FIVE:

Summer

Then we had another phone call.

Our social worker told us we had been matched with a little girl—who was fourteen months old. She had blue eyes and short, wispy hair. She'd been in foster care most of her life, first with her birth mother, then alone once they had decided to place her away from her family. She was attached to her foster family, and there weren't any medical issues.

We hugged and cried again. I think that moment, alongside our wedding day, was the happiest I'd ever been in my life.

We met that week to look at the file—and we got to see a blurry picture (cute, but she looked a bit like a boy as she had very little hair).

Another amazing surprise was that she had a little brother who was four months old (we saw a squashed baby picture of him—looking a lot like his sister). He had a file too—as Summer was looked after, they were watching the family closely and he'd been placed with both birth parents in a home that assessed their parenting—and theoretically helped keep him safe.

He was exactly one year younger than her and had been

conceived and born whilst they were assessing them and removing Summer. I can't imagine a more stressful situation—apart from living in a war zone or being pregnant and homeless. It must have been terrible for them.

At the time we weren't thinking about that at all—just about Summer and Christopher, and our possible new family. "Would you like to go ahead?" Our social worker had to ask—but she could tell by our giant grins. She set up the blind viewing of Summer and accompanied us due to our past experience.

We met the foster mum and Summer in her home about an hours drive from ours. We could tell that the foster mum was really emotionally attached to her. Summer acted like a normal little girl—toddling around as she had only just learned how to walk. She liked a noisy toy where you put balls in the top…they went around a tree and came out the bottom—so we played with that for ages. There was a massive Rottweiler that barked and then lay down in the middle of the floor. Summer was completely used to him—she patted and whacked him, and he didn't seem to mind. It was surreal.

Summer came outside to wave us off, and our social worker checked again whether we wanted to proceed—"YES."

The next step was to go to the panel again. It was similar to last time but focused mostly on Summer. It went well and we met with the child's social worker to discuss "Introductions," the handover period where you

Part One: Jane's Story

take increasing responsibility for the child until they are finally "Placed" in your home. Ours was to take two weeks.

We had a few days to prepare—we had to buy a cot, tell the family, squeal and dance around the lounge. Fortunately, we were both self-employed—which meant that we could be flexible and take time off. However, it did also mean that we didn't get any maternity leave, or pay from anyone.

We started visiting the foster carers house and taking Summer out to the park. Then they brought her over to our house for a visit, and eventually, she stayed overnight. After two weeks we were all exhausted from the travel and emotion. We also hadn't been told that her routine was getting up at 4 a.m. every day. Fortunately, we are morning people—but this took a bit of getting used to.

She didn't sleep very well, and of course, it was very stressful on her as this was her second big move, and the first she could remember. Her foster family were her family, so she was confused and upset. We'd never had children full time, so it was relentless and tiring—even with two of us. But it went well.

The foster family had looked after her for ten months and really struggled to let go emotionally. Had they been younger, they would have no doubt adopted Summer themselves. But they did an amazing job, and we are really grateful to them for the fantastic caring job they did for Summer and us.

We were still involved with the social workers—she would visit every few days to check we were doing okay. It was no doubt to help us, and they did give us some good advice, but it felt like an intrusion and an added pressure to demonstrate we were "coping". We got the hang of the logistics, but Summer cried a lot and continued sleeping poorly. It was a huge transition for her—and she couldn't talk or really understand what was going on. We started going to toddler groups and everyone assumed I'd given birth. Those early days were amazing, exciting, exhausting, and sometimes terrible.

You are taught to make the attachment with the child before you really let the family get too involved. This was really hard for our parents, as she was the first grandchild and they couldn't really understand why they couldn't look after her.

Summer attached to me really quickly but rejected David. It was exhausting for me, as she only wanted me to look after her…and demoralising for him. He spoke to another Dad in our boot camp group, who had experienced the same thing. He suggested having some one-to-one time with Summer when Jane wasn't around. So David started bathing Summer on his own, which did help a little. I was still number one though. In fact, I was "Mumma" and so was he. It reminded me of that kid's dinosaur program where there was "Mumma" and "not da Mumma". At least he was Mumma.

Part One: Jane's Story

CHAPTER SIX:

Christopher

Whilst this was happening Christopher was moving through the system. The birth family was still not deemed to be suitable carers, and we were told we could proceed with him. We met him at his foster carers house (not the same as Summer's).

He was a GORGEOUS ten months old baby. We took Summer with us, and she was fine. Christopher spent the time biting a table and crawling around at a hundred miles per hour. They had an open plan house, and he scooted around in a baby walker, bashing into everything. He liked wheels and cars. Again our social worker came with us, and we gave her the thumbs up.

We didn't have to go to the Adoption Panel again, fortunately, as they had put the kids through as a bundle deal. We planned and started Introductions. Christopher was fine and seemed nonplussed by the whole situation.

You could see that lightbulb moment when Summer realised that Christopher was more than just a visitor. She was 22 months at the time and had an anxious attachment style. If you've read any books on attachment, you'd recognise that she saw her attachment to me (in particular) under threat—so her behaviour deteriorated.

Halfway through the Introductions, we were due to have a meeting with both Christopher's and our social worker, to see how it was all going. That morning Summer started throwing up. We were fairly sure that it was stress, but I made an emergency appointment with our GP. She and I missed the meeting. David went—and in fact carried on with Christopher's Introductions, and took point with Christopher, as all of my energy was spent managing Summer's emotions.

The social workers were concerned—and suggested pausing Introductions. We told them we just wanted to get on with it—as it was far more stressful for everyone with the toing and froing. We did, and Christopher moved in just before Christmas.

The next six months were probably the most stressful of my life. Going from one child to two in only six months was a steep learning curve—but Summer was jealous and began acting out. Multiple tantrums a day and terrible sleep. She wouldn't eat in the same room as him, so we resorted to me feeding Summer in the lounge, and David feeding Christopher in the kitchen.

It was amazing, and terrible at the same time. Christmas came, and we bought them little red outfits to wear. It was a very special day—although Summer ate too much chocolate and wouldn't sleep. She kept screaming for hours. We have some great photos of that first Christmas though—including one of Summer eating that huge chocolate bunny.

In February we went to court to adopt Summer. It was

Part One: Jane's Story

a low-key event, but we dressed up. The judge was lovely.

We were making progress with the adoption. We had social worker visits, and Christopher seemed fine. Summer hit a turning point after six months of Christopher living with us, and settled down a bit. Although we still couldn't leave her alone in the same room as him, as we didn't trust her not to hurt him.

Christopher learned to walk and chase our cat. We went on holiday with my parents in a cottage in Suffolk. Summer was learning to talk, Christopher was very charming and made funny faces.

* * *

In August we adopted Christopher and we were "signed off" by social services. We heaved a huge sigh of relief. They are generally lovely people, and they want what is best for the children—but it is hard living under a microscope. We were officially "good enough". Now we just had to keep them alive until adulthood; stop our relationship from failing, and retain and our sanity.

From here on out, were on our own. We went to toddler groups, to make friends with other parents. My sister also had a daughter that was exactly a year younger than Christopher. She decided that one was fine for her—so all the grandchildren were done.

Summer started a couple of mornings a week at pre-school, where she loved to paint. She was very clingy, but it gave me some time alone with Christopher.

We started to notice that some of Christopher's behaviour was strange. He LOVED cars, wheels, transport, and putting things into ordered lines. He'd always made funny faces, but when he was stable enough to walk, he started running up and down the hallway flapping his ears for twenty minutes at a time. We left him to it, as he seemed to enjoy it—but searched on Google. It said that flapping was an autism trait, so we panicked a bit.

Further research gave me the term "Sensory Integration Disorder" as a subset of autism. I noticed that Adoption UK was doing a one day course on it, so I signed David and I up. SID is apparently far more prevalent in adopted children—although they don't really know why, or what it's cause actually is. Trauma in pregnancy possibly—which certainly fit Christopher's history. So we went along.

We learned a lot that day—and definitely recognised a lot of the behaviours in Christopher. They recommended us a company that could diagnose the disorder. Although it cost a few hundred pounds, we booked an appointment and went along. It was like an occupational therapy session, with swinging, squashing, rolling and fine motor skills testing. Christopher loved it—and although he was only three years old, they diagnosed him. They explained what it meant for him…and I went out and bought another pile of books.

This is how I explain it to people: we all have a certain amount of processing power in our brain (like a computer RAM). Christopher's body does not

Part One: Jane's Story

automatically know where is arms, legs and body are. He has poor balance and is also sensitive to noises. A big chunk of Christopher's brain-power (say thirty per cent) is spent on finding and moving his arms and legs, keeping his balance and dealing with noises. It leaves less brainpower for concentrating and learning. He likes to move around and finds it difficult to have others in his personal space unless he invites it. He finds loud noises like fire alarms and hand dryers scary—but is happy being noisy himself. In fact, he has developed a fire engine noise that is extremely realistic and has people looking around for an engine.

The flapping is a way for him to regulate himself, and give him sensory input. When I ask him about it now, he says he enjoys it—although he is starting to become more embarrassed about it, and is trying to replace it with vigorous tickle play with me.

We also noticed that Christopher seemed younger than his peers. It was lovely when he was a baby—as we both got to do a bit more baby parenting. When he started pre-school at age two and a half, we had a chat with his key-worker and established that he was tracking behind his classmates both intellectually and socially. He acted more like the two-year-olds, than his three-year-old peers.

* * *

Christopher was nearly five years old when he started Infants school. He was just about potty trained during the day but acted like a three-year-old. Christopher has always been confident. He makes friends easily (although they are immature relationships with uncomplicated children).

We had chosen an outstanding school a mile away, rather than the closer one that seemed apathetic. I didn't think they would make the effort to help my son, so we used our rights as adopters to get him into the better school, and I'm grateful that we did. I set up a joint meeting with his keyworkers at the pre-school, and the Year R teacher and SENCO at his new school, to aid with the transition.

Over Year R and Year One at school, he progressed about a year behind—but we were hopeful that he'd catch up. Once he started year two it became clear that they needed to give him a lot more help—the lessons were too advanced for his current development level. He was bored and not improving. So the teachers and I decided that we would apply for an Education, Health and Care (EHC) Needs Assessment—which used to be called a "statement." It was a lot of work for the teachers, and I am really grateful to them for their effort.

He saw a host of healthcare professionals, including an Occupational Therapist (OT), Speech and Language person, Educational Psychologist, and Developmental Paediatrician. We'd been working with some of these for a few years through the NHS and the school. They wrote a number of reports for his assessments. They diagnosed him with mild Autism, which wasn't much of a surprise. He was deemed to need a full-time person to help him at school. It was close to the wire, but we managed to get it done at the end of the school's Year

Two, and before he started at his new Junior school.

Our Adoption Adventure

Part One: Jane's Story

CHAPTER SEVEN:

Moving Forward

Summer started at infants school, and although highly reluctant to do any homework, she did fine. She's quite shy, but made some good friends and was happy to go to school most of the time. She still verges on clingy, and under stress, she always wants me rather than David.

Christopher has turned into a bit of a ladies man. He's always been charming—that's his way of coping with developing new attachments to different mother figures. He was in a mother and baby foster carer placement until he was six months old, and then in foster care for four months, whilst he waited for his court judgement to come through. At birthday parties and toddler groups, he's always searched for the prettiest young lady in a room and tried to get her attention—even at ten months. I think he was trying to find someone to look after him—and the behaviour has stuck. Now aged seven, he is one of the few that have started to have girlfriends at school—we'll need to keep an eye on that with the teachers, as he gets older!

We exchange a letter with the children's birth mother once a year, where I let her know how Summer and Christopher have been getting on—we plan to share these letters with our children when they are mature enough to be able to understand them. Our children's birth mother separated from their birth father soon after Christopher had been removed, and nobody has a forwarding address for him. Letters are sent via the council to keep our addresses private.

She subsequently had another baby with a new partner, and our social worker asked us whether or not we would be willing to take on a third child. My kids would have been three and four at the time, so it would have been a big ask—but we seriously considered it. It turned out that the new area she was living in had a far less aggressive approach to adoption, and the guidelines for removing children had become stricter, so she was allowed to keep that child—and the next one as well.

I feel for those children and hope their mother is in a better place now than she was when they assessed her for Summer and Christopher. They feel like my blood—as they share my children's blood, and I hope that they can escape from the cycle of inadequate parenting.

My parents moved further away from us, and after a year of long drives to see them, we decided to move closer. We didn't take the decision lightly as it would mean moving county and schools. I knew that Summer would struggle to make new friends and Christopher would need a new team of specialists.

We decided to time it with Christopher's school move, between Infants and Junior school. We chose a mainstream school with a caring staff and a can-do attitude, which we could work with to support both of them. I've found it necessary to be pleasant, but fairly insistent on setting meetings with teachers and staff when I feel it necessary. Part of the adoption process is to actually make sure you are willing to be a "squeaky wheel" and get your children the help they need—when they need it. Fortunately, I am pretty good at that!

We moved a couple of months ago, and it was as traumatic as I thought it would be. The whole period from deciding to move, selling the house, waiting, moving and starting a new school was stressful for the kids (and us). I think it was the correct decision though, as we are spending more time with our family. Behaviour has been very challenging from them both, but we are hoping that they will make some good friendships and settle down in time.

Our Adoption Adventure

Part Two: David's Story

CHAPTER EIGHT:

My Childhood

I've been apprehensive about sharing my adoption story.

It features a lot of pain, so I try to keep things private and rarely talk about it with friends. Men are also not the best at opening up their feelings, so I've not been looking forward to getting pen to paper.

Where to start? I grew up on the outskirts of a large town. My father was a Senior Charge Nurse at the local hospital, and my mother was a nurse at a care home. I went to a junior school about five minutes walk from house.

My sister was born when I was six. I became the compliant, shy child, and my sister was the defiant extrovert.

My father was a strict disciplinarian and ruled with a slipper. I remember trying to be helpful by getting my fathers camera bag out of the cupboard…I dropped it and it broke. I was afraid to tell him.

We didn't have a lot of money when I was younger. Most things were second hand, they couldn't afford to send me to clubs, and holidays were usually spent camping, as they couldn't afford to stay at resorts or go abroad.

The upside was that I spent a lot of time outdoors. Parenting wasn't as cautious about safety back then. My next-door neighbour was in the same class as me at junior school, and the two of us often spent hours wandering about the woods together at the weekend…only returning home when we were hungry. I also had a blunt hatchet, which I used to chop the stump of a holly tree in my garden—I don't think I ever finished that job!

* * *

Fast-forward a few years, and by the time I was twenty-four, I'd graduated university with a degree in Computer Science, an MBA, and had moved back to live with my parents. I worked as a Marketing Executive at a nearby Publishing company. I hadn't learned how to save money at that point, so I spent all my earnings on my car (a brand new red BMW 3 series compact which I couldn't afford), and I spent all the rest of my wages on nights out with friends. I think upon reflection, that I was using my spending to overcompensate for feelings of being poor as a young child.

"Can you give me a lift to the shops?" asked my younger sister one Saturday. "Sure." I put on my Giorgio Armani suit overcoat—it was another extravagant indulgence on my salary; navy blue, single-breasted and finished just above my knees.

We got in the car and drove off. "Oh, and I've invited some friends along." I rolled my eyes—she always liked to spring surprises on me. We pulled up at a house, and the girls bundled into the back of my car. "David, this is Jane." "Hi." She was beautiful, with long blonde hair, blue eyes and a pale complexion.

I spent the day walking around the shops with the girls and got to know Jane a little more. I was 24 at the time. She had just turned 18 and was studying for her A-Levels. She enjoyed spending time outdoors, reading, sci-fi and delicious food. She also intended to go to university. We were both meticulous planners and had a lot in common.

A few days later I invited her out to a quaint little teashop, for a cream tea. It was meant to be a date, but I was feeling so shy about asking her out, that I brought my sister with me. I know, pretty dumb idea. We talked and talked, but of course, she had no idea it was a date at all. I was getting nowhere.

My sister helped me to devise a 'cunning plan'. I was to be elsewhere with my friends that evening. My sister went out with Jane and a group of friends partying on New Year's Eve.

She told Jane that she'd lined up someone special for her kiss that evening. Just as the clock turned midnight I drove over to meet her for that special kiss…my heart was pounding. "Would she already be with someone else?" "Maybe she isn't interested in me at all?" A wave of doubt washed over me. She gave me a long kiss, and the rest we say is history.

Jane later told me "You got me with your car and coat—you should have just asked me out."

We became inseparable. We spent our weekends together, and I also came over some evenings after work. We wrote each other love letters, enjoyed visiting National Trust properties and eating out together. George Michael's song "Fast Love" was often playing on the radio when we were driving around in my BMW—the song always reminds me of our early dates. Her college was a short walk to my office, so we often met at lunchtime for a picnic in the local park during the summer.

As we both liked to plan, we often had long discussions about our future. We wanted to get married at some point, and both aspired to have two children.

I spent more and more time with her...and she spent less and less time studying. Unfortunately, her A-Level exams didn't go as well as she planned. But her grades were just good enough to get her into university to study biochemistry.

She went on holiday with her family around that time, and they'd asked me to check on their cat, which was old and had seen better days. Unfortunately, I discovered the cat lifeless, in a cardboard box. I had to deliver the sad news.

Part Two: David's Story

Jane would be living at the university in only a couple of month's time—an hour and a quarter from me. Like many people enjoying romance at this stage in their lives, we wondered what would happen next? Could our relationship endure?

Neither of us wanted to break up. So we set a schedule for me to drive down after work on Wednesday, to stay the night—then get up early to drive to work on Thursday morning. I next came back down again on Friday night and left for work on Monday morning. So I effectively saw her nearly every day of the week. I'll never know how we managed to sleep in that impossibly small student bed; you had to stay in one position all night, as there was no room to turn over.

* * *

At the end of her first year at university, things were getting serious, so we decided to move in together. Her parents were looking to invest some money in property, so they bought a flat near the university and we rented it from them. One of the first purchases on our list was a double bed.

I'd rented houses with friends when I was at university, but this was the first time either of us had lived with a partner. We could hardly contain our excitement when we moved in and decided to decorate…we didn't know any better, so we sponge painted multi-coloured shells and seahorses on the side of the bath, painted acrylic clouds on the lounge wall, and many other decorating faux pas I'd rather forget.

Having to be responsible for paying the bills, I started saving, rather than spending all my wages. I planned to save up a deposit to buy a house.

I carried on commuting to work, but it could often take up to two hours if the traffic was bad. I was feeling drained all the time, so I got a new job with a nearby financial services company, which was both a promotion and an increase in salary.

Our next two years were blissful. Jane finished her degree with a good grade and started working. I was 29, and she was 23. Like most couples who've been together for many years, we'd had the occasional pregnancy scare when her period was late, but they were all false alarms. We were so relieved, at the time, and thought how strange it was that those people who'd got a job straight out of school already had children of their own. "Those silly people." Little did we know what the future held for us…

* * *

I got another promotion. With as much savings as we could muster and a little help from our parents, we bought our first house. It was a tiny one-bedroom cottage, with a study. We had to donate of most of the furniture from our previous flat, as nothing fit. The house was on a busy road, with a bus stop directly outside. You had to be careful to close the bedroom curtains when you were getting undressed, as the people on the upper floor of the bus could see right into our bedroom!

Part Two: David's Story

We went to a last chance animal sanctuary and adopted our first pet—a ginger cat called Tigger. He was a really loving cat and liked to sit on us all the time, purring. We kept Tigger inside, as we were worried he'd get hit by a car on the busy road outside our house—but he was desperate to go out. Once I put a long, retractable cat harness on him to let him explore outside...he immediately ran up a tree, and I spent the next twenty minutes with my arm stuck in the air, trying to encourage him to come back down.

Jane got a job in the lab of a miscarriage clinic. She met a lot of sad mothers to be, who were finding it difficult to have a child. She started getting broody for a baby. Being in the industry, she knew that biologically speaking it was better to have a child now, rather than to keep waiting. Her 'clock' was ticking. We'd been together for five years, and Jane was in 'nesting mode.'

"So when are you going to marry me?" became a familiar question. I kept telling her we should wait until we had more money, a bigger house, and so on...

* * *

Two years later, we'd decided it was really time to get a larger house. We were looking at the properties on the market, when Jane discovered her childhood home was for sale—a four-bedroom townhouse.

It wasn't in the town we wanted to live in, but we decided to go and see it out of curiosity. It brought back a flood of happy childhood memories for her. The house still had the same kitchen her father installed over twenty years ago; the familiar brick effect wallpaper in the living room, and the snug where her father had kept his model railway. We weren't planning to live in that area, but in the end, we purchased it out of sentiment. Tigger liked it, as he finally had his own cat flap and could go outside.

I'd been putting off getting married, but I felt I was out of excuses with this new house, as her parents had raised two children in it. We wouldn't even be using two of the rooms. So we finally set a date for the wedding. She was 23 and I was 30 years old.

Having spent most of our money purchasing the house, we had a very small wedding with only 3 friends and immediate family. That decision caused a lot of friction with our extended family and friends, and it became a really stressful time, as they all complained. So much so, that we considered eloping abroad.

Once we were married, Jane kept asking about having a baby. I'd always pictured having two children, but just like the decision to get married, I'd kept putting it off…"Just one more year…babies are expensive…let's save some more money first."

Four more years went by…

* * *

I was now 34 and Jane was 27 years old. Jane was working locally and I was exhausted by the commuting and business trips. I decided to do contract work from home, so we could spend more time together. We

Part Two: David's Story

bought a small two-bedroom bungalow in the town that we'd wanted to live in for years. Property in the area was more expensive, so the new house cost more than our previous four-bedroom house, even though it was only half the size.

Unfortunately, our beloved first cat 'Tigger" died. We thought he was around sixteen years old, so it was probably old age. We were both very sad, and Jane cried a lot.

A week later, an unknown ginger cat came through our cat flap and started sleeping in our house. It spent most of the day and night with us, so we wondered whether he had an owner. There wasn't a collar. We started to get worried whether he was getting fed, so we started giving him food. We didn't know his name, so we called him 'Mr Kat.' We went to the vet to have him checked out. They told us that he'd lived with one owner until she had a baby, then moved in with someone else—they had a baby, so he sought us out. Accordingly, we unofficially adopted him. It was nice having a cat again, and he lessened the grief we felt from Tigger dying.

Our Adoption Adventure

Part Two: David's Story

CHAPTER NINE:

Is That Semen in Your Pocket?

After a lot of convincing, I finally gave in and we decided to try for a baby. We attempted for three months without success. But those were fun months with plenty of sex at random times.

Then we discovered an ovulation website on the Internet and tried to time her most fertile periods. All the fun went out of sex—it became a job. I felt like I was a sex doll. "Hurry up." I was just being used for one-minute sex before and after work; afterwards, she'd put a pillow under her bottom, and lie on her back with her legs in the air. For some reason, it always reminded me of a chicken in the grocery aisle.

Every month her period came. Every month I could see the distress in her eyes. Jane's mother often called to check whether she was pregnant—I could hear her Mum's disappointment when they spoke on the phone. I felt very sorry for Jane, and the amount of pressure she was under.

Her periods were usually accompanied by a lot of pain. She spent the morning lying down, with a hot water bottle, and some painkillers. This was 'normal' for her.

Our Adoption Adventure

"What's wrong with us? Why couldn't we get pregnant?" We ate reasonably healthily; we exercised three times a week; we didn't smoke.

After one year of trying we felt we had waited long enough, and booked an appointment to discuss it with our doctor. Jane was only 27 and apparently fit and healthy. I was 33.

Jane had some blood tests and examinations.

I had to do a sperm test. I remember masturbating at home, into a specimen tube. I was worried that if I missed it would go everywhere! And I couldn't afford to miss a drop. When you orgasm it feels like a flood of fluid coming out of your body—it's disappointing when you discover that's its only about a teaspoon of liquid.

Following the doctor's instructions, I put the tube of semen into my trouser pocket, to keep it warm. Then I drove to the hospital to hand it in for testing. I felt really self-conscious walking around the hospital. It was silly, but I wondered whether people could tell I had semen in my pocket?

Another week or two later, we had a follow-up meeting with our doctor to discuss our lab results. I felt like I was getting on in years, and had started to wonder whether my sperm was deteriorating. "You have good sperm mobility, shape and volume," said the doctor. I let out a quiet sigh of relief. It was selfish, but I felt thankful that I was not the problem.

Jane's lab results were also ok. The doctor referred us to

Part Two: David's Story

a special clinic for further investigation, and possibly IVF. If approved, we would be allowed one cycle of IVF, free of charge. After that, we would need to pay if we wanted to do more rounds. Each cycle cost around £2,500 at the time.

We made many visits to the clinic, where Jane underwent different tests. Each time there was a procedure, we had to wait another month or two to get the results and book another appointment. This took months, and months. They decided to do a laparoscopy on Jane, to see if they could find any reason why she had had difficulty getting pregnant—we had to wait seven months for the surgery. The hospital discovered she had endometriosis, and informed us that IVF was our only choice to get pregnant.

We went for another consultation, and they told us they had one of the highest success rates in the county (up to 50%), so we were filled to the brim with confidence.

Jane was then given three months of drugs to trick the body into thinking it was in menopause, to reduce some of the endometriosis. The first round of drugs didn't work properly, so she had to take stronger ones. She didn't have much fun with all the hot flushes, and soaked bedclothes.

After that, she was given drugs to hyper-stimulate her ovaries, so that she produced more eggs than normal. She found this part of the process really painful. She was then given a hormonal injection a couple of days before she went into surgery to have her eggs extracted.

Our Adoption Adventure

I had to donate my half of the deal on the same day. I was led to a small room with a comfy chair, a waist height padded table, and a selection of adult magazines to choose from. It was an awkward experience. Knowing that other men had ejaculated all over the place, it was difficult to choose whether to lie down, sit, stand, and let's not get started on touching the magazines!

I turned around to bolt the door and found there wasn't a lock. "That's reassuring!" And then there was the pressure…I had to produce the sperm now! Everyone was counting on me. In the end, I decided to lie down, as I was becoming too anxious, and didn't think I'd be able to 'get it up' if I kept stressing about the situation.

I closed my eyes….click. What's that noise? Did the door handle turn?…" I opened my eyes and turned my body away from the door.

"No, it's just me being paranoid." I lay back and closed my eyes again.

"Okay, focus, focus. You can do it…"

After longer than I'd have liked, I finally managed to make my donation into the tube. It didn't look like much, but there it was—my half of the baby.

A couple of days later, we went back to the clinic. The doctor reminded us, "We're inserting multiple embryos, so there is the possibility you could give birth to twins." That was fine with us—we could get our two children in one go!

Part Two: David's Story

All we had to do was cross our fingers and wait…

* * *

Jane used a home pregnancy test kit, and it looked as though she was pregnant—but two weeks later the familiar crimson wave appeared. Jane cried. I felt like I'd had the wind knocked out of me.

We had a follow-up appointment with the clinic, and another scan to see why IVF hadn't succeeded. Jane went in for an MRI, and they discovered that the endometriosis was more extensive than they'd initially thought. It was "stage four," the worst kind. The endometriosis had gummed up her ovaries, bowel, and all of her pelvic region. Her anatomy was out of alignment.

Endometriosis was the reason why she suffered so much pain during her period. It was the reason why she only had a bowel movement every two to three days.

It was the reason we couldn't have children.

We asked them what we should do next. They told us that Jane could have surgery to have the endometriosis removed, but there was no guarantee she would have a successful round of IVF. The IVF drugs would also aggravate the endometriosis. On top of that, the surgery would likely cause more adhesions, and the endometriosis would probably grow back. So once she had an operation, she could expect multiple surgeries for the rest of her life. The procedure could also go badly, and she might end up having a colostomy, or worse.

Or, we could decide to do nothing, and leave the endo alone. She might be lucky and never need to have surgery.

It was a big decision. So they asked us to spend some time considering our options.

Our next appointment got delayed until after Christmas. We spent the period researching endometriosis surgery and IVF. When we went back for our appointment, we finally decided that it was too risky for Jane's health to do the surgery, especially as the chances of her getting pregnant were so small.

We signed a form to say that we didn't want to keep our embryos. That was the final 'nail in the coffin'. We couldn't have children.

Jane spent many months crying in the foetal position. Every time we saw a baby, or anything related to babies, she fell into despair and broke down in tears. We had both suffered a loss—the babies we wouldn't have. She felt she wasn't a woman anymore. Her reason for 'being' was gone.

The clinic recommended we see one of their counsellors for therapy. I thought it would be a waste of time, but it turned out to be really useful. The counsellor helped us to realise that it was okay to grieve.

The counsellor asked Jane to write her feelings in a

Part Two: David's Story

diary each day. She preferred to journal in private, and kept it hidden in a drawer.

Jane went off sex. When we did have intercourse, it was a mentally painful reminder of her infertility. She only did it for me.

A few months went by, and Jane could finally look at a baby without crying. But every time we heard that someone was pregnant, she felt resentment about how 'easy' it was for them.

Once we started opening up to friends about having trouble getting pregnant, we were surprised to discover that a lot of others had also had problems, but they kept it very private. Many of the women we knew had miscarried before. Others had got pregnant with IVF. Another couple we knew had done seven rounds of IVF, before giving up.

One woman we knew had the dilemma of choosing either her baby's health…or hers. The medications she was on would harm a baby, but coming off them would harm her. In the end, she decided she would have a baby, despite the risks.

Our Adoption Adventure

Part Two: David's Story

CHAPTER TEN:

Under a Magnifying Glass

We both still wanted to have children but weren't sure which route to take next. We considered surrogacy, but it didn't seem to be that common in the UK. You couldn't legally pay the surrogate for the baby, only their expenses. So there was the possibility of spending a lot of money, with not much more than a promise from the surrogate…and maybe she would decide to keep the baby for herself.

We next looked at adoption and attended a free seminar run by the county council. There were about thirty people in the room, mostly women. The presentation gave a brief overview of the process, and then told you how awful it could be, in order to thin out the less committed people in the audience. We were desperate and determined to proceed, so we signed up.

Once we get started on a particular course of action, we like to fully immerse ourselves—so we bought and read numerous books on adoption, we subscribed to Adoption UK and went to a number of adoption events.

A few months later our council held an adoption preparation course, taking two days a week for the next four weeks. There were four couples including us, plus two single women.

We were an eclectic group of thirty and fortysomethings, which at first glance had nothing in common. But, because we had to share intimate secrets with each other during the workshop exercises, the 'Prep Group' bonded together, and we all made friends for life—Jane calls it 'Boot camp'. We had to be willing to change our views on all aspects of parenting, to open up to each other, and expose our emotional vulnerabilities.

We met one couple that had already spent a year going through the adoption process for China. But they told us that after they got approved, they discovered that the waitlist for children from China was many years—so they'd decided to switch to UK adoption instead. Disappointingly, the paperwork and training weren't transferable, so they still had to go through another year to become UK adopters.

Every day was emotionally draining. I kept a reflective diary of those four weeks...

Week 1
What did I learn today about myself?
- After drawing a timeline of my life, I could see that the majority of the key events had happened to me from the age of 18 onwards. I couldn't recall many significant events from my primary school years—which meant I'd had a happy and stable childhood. This would contrast with an adoptee, who would have had many traumatic events in their early years.

Part Two: David's Story

What did I learn about Jane?
- That Jane's Mum earned more than her Dad at one point.

What did I learn about adoption?
- I'd read a lot of books and magazines on adoption before starting the prep day, had spoken with adopters, and attended external events.
- The themes were similar, however the points I wasn't particularly aware of before this were:
    - You shouldn't change the first name of a baby, no matter how young they are (unless it puts the baby in danger).
    - Adoption from inter-country adoption from China can take up to 10 years!
    - The Iceberg Model—messages/lessons from childhood leaking out into behaviours.

How do I feel after today's session
- Very excited to be officially starting the process now and looking forward to the next prep training day. I hope to make some good friends from the group.

Week 2
What did I learn about the child's route to adoption?
- The legal process for Care Proceedings takes much longer than I first thought…40 weeks.

- Very few children are put up for adoption voluntarily. Most cases are due to a collection of factors rather than one single factor. e.g. neglect + alcohol + violence + abuse, etc.

What did I learn about attachment and its importance in adoption?
- The "Sculpt" exercise with the string was very powerful. It really brought home to me how attachments are being made and broken multiple times, causing confusion and frustration for the child. This also makes the child more unwilling to create future attachments.

What did I learn about child development?
- Drawing from Maslow's Hierarchy of Needs, we could see that many of the critical foundation blocks may have been missing after the child's birth, affecting their behaviour in future years.

What was the biggest surprise about today's session?
- That Care Proceedings take so long—this makes me very sad for the child, as they may get moved around a few times during this, and will gain and lose attachments multiple times. The child's discomfort may be prolonged.

How do I feel after today's session?
- It was a really depressing day. Being bombarded with negative themes all day left me feeling drained.

Week 3
What things worry me most about the decisions to be made when being considered for a child?

- I feel that if we wait too long, our criteria might continue widening in desperation, and we will take on a child that we might regret later.

- Given the unknown things that happen to these children, and the alcohol/drugs the mother might have taken during pregnancy, I worry that we might take on a child that seems okay, only to later discover a serious physical disability.

What have I learned about the difficulties that a new parent might expect?

- There may be some habits that they enjoy, but I may disapprove of—such as eating fast food every day. We will need to gradually wean them off their habits in the long term, not all at once.

- We will constantly need to be adapting our behaviour to the child. Perhaps they will flinch when you raise your hand (as they think you will hit them). Or maybe they are used to lots of noise, and can't sleep when it's quiet. It will be a constant cycle of observing and understanding their behaviour.

What do I think are the most important reasons for a child to maintain some form of contact with their birth family?

- Even though they may have had traumatic experiences with their birth parents, they may still love them. There is likely to be some attachment, particularly with an older child who has been in their care for many years. It can be more traumatic to break the bond.

- I've also listened to and read about adoptees that have built an angelic view of their birth parents in their mind, as they have not been told the gory details. We plan to tell our children.

What are going to be the greatest challenges for me in maintaining such contact?

- After reading the Child's Permanence Report, I am likely to feel anger towards the parents over how they could take such poor care of their child. My first impulse would be to get the child far away from their parents, so I can protect them from their emotional and physical trauma. I would also be concerned about how upset they might get meeting them face-to-face.

- However, my practical side tells me that it is important they still keep some attachments from their old life, so some level of contact should be actively encouraged (unless it puts the child in danger).

Week 4
What have I learned about the qualities needed to parent an adopted child?

- Displaying the PACE (Play, Acceptance, Curiosity, Empathy) qualities when playing with them helps to make the play time much more fun and lets them use their imagination. I have learned that you shouldn't correct your child or get them to conform to the real world when playing with them. There was a great example in the workshop of the child playing with a toy car (and then pretending it was something else). You also need the PACE qualities in general parenting, in order to understand why they display problem behaviours and help them to regulate their emotions.

- I have a lot of empathy and curiosity. I spend a time playing with children, but this could be increased with more babysitting or going to a nursery. Accepting the child's behaviours will be the hardest challenge, which will improve with practice.

In thinking about what I have learned over the last four weeks, how am I feeling about my application to become an adoptive parent?
- I'm still very keen to adopt and want to get through all the forms and steps at a hundred miles an hour! I'm not put off by what I have learned and I'm eager to start having my forever family.

Describe one thing that I'm looking forward to, and one thing that terrifies me about the road ahead?
- I'm looking forward to playing with the child/children and teaching them new things.

- I'm terrified that we will give a lot of love, but what if the child never loves us back?

* * *

At home, Mr Kat got really sick and Jane took him to the vets. They said all his organs were failing and they would need to put him down. Jane came back in tears without him. Remembering how we got over the grief of our previous cat, we bought a grey kitten in the next couple of weeks, which we named River.

Soon we were assigned a Social worker to help us through the adoption process. The checks made to become an approved adopter are extensive. Anyone who successfully gets through will feel like a super-parent by the end of it.

What followed was a whole year of regular meetings at our home, and lots of homework and form filling in-between. It was really stressful. Although the Social worker is there to help you through the process, you're also aware that she's evaluating you every time she meets you. Whenever we gave a detail about our life, she'd drill further and further into it, to get behind our feelings.

One task Jane and I had to do was decide what range of children's backgrounds we were willing to accept. Children are taken into care for all sorts of reasons. It could be neglect or abuse; the mother could have been on drugs and alcohol whilst pregnant; the child could be disabled or possibly have autism, but they may be too young for a concrete diagnosis. You have to decide your criteria and attempt to stick to it.

Jane and I decided we could accept neglect, but abuse was only a 'maybe', depending on the specifics. We felt that we enjoyed being physically active, so a disabled

Part Two: David's Story

child wouldn't be the right fit for us.

We both had to have a full medical check-up, and were DBS checked to ensure we were not unsuitable to be around children.

They wanted us to both have childcare experience, so Jane got a part-time job at a pre-school nursery, looking after children between three months and five years old.

I spent a couple of hours a week volunteering at a Sure Start centre and focused on playing with children of different ages and genders. On top of that, we babysat our neighbour's little boy most weeks, at no charge. One of the guys in our Prep Group started to volunteer at a kids football club, to gain experience with slightly older children—he thought he was more likely to get a five-year-old than a baby, as he was older than us.

I thought it was overkill to get so much childcare experience—although retrospectively, I'm really glad we did. If all pregnant mums got a few months of experience of looking after babies before they gave birth, it would really help them when their child was born. It's a shame that in the UK, new mums are given very little training when they give birth.

We had to share our financial information with them, to prove we could afford to look after a child. We showed them our income, monthly expenses, bank statements and assets. It was very invasive. Social Services would ideally like one or both of you to become stay at home parents, so that you can spend more time bonding with your adopted child. Of course, this has to be balanced with being able to afford to do that.

We told close family and a small circle of friends that we were going through the adoption process. It was unavoidable, as part of the process included a social worker interviewing a family member and two friends, to see what they thought about you…and whether they thought you would make suitable parents. Even though these people should have your best interests in mind, it was still nerve-wracking waiting to find out whether our Social worker was happy with their responses; or if the information raised any issues.

We were asked to draw a line showing all the major events in our lives, such as jobs, moving home, pets, deaths and so on, so that they could ask us to reflect on how those events shaped us, and how they might affect our parenting styles.

Not all of our meetings were together. Jane and I had to be interviewed separately to talk about the strength of our relationship and the qualities we provided to each other.

The social worker also conducted a health and safety assessment of our house. It included obvious things such as making sure any medications or chemicals were up high or behind child locked doors; ensuring all glass was safety glass (we had to get a few things replaced after that); to whether rooms had sufficient light for a child to read and play in.

* * *

Part Two: David's Story

Finally, twelve months of paperwork and assessments had been completed. We both had nearly a year's experience of looking after children. It was time to go to the Adoption Panel, to approve us for adoption—It's like getting a license to say you're 'good enough' to adopt.

To say we were nervous was an understatement. We sat in a holding room with our social worker, waiting to be called. My heart was racing. My hands were clammy. I was sweating.

Someone asked us to come in. There was a large rectangle of desks, with about a dozen people sitting about ten feet away from us on the other side. The gap between them and us felt imposing. We were being judged. The panel was a mixture of social workers, a lawyer, doctor, foster carers, past adopters and people who had been adopted themselves. They introduced themselves, then looked through our application form and asked questions.

Afterwards, Jane and I were led back to the holding room to await the judgement, along with our social worker…

Although our social worker had done her best to prepare us for the panel, we knew there was no guarantee. One of our friends had been to the panel and was rejected—they appealed the decision, and eventually had two little girls placed with them, but it was a long and tortuous journey.

There are many reasons why you could get rejected,

such as the panel may feel you aren't over the grief of not having children; the three family and friends you asked the social worker to interview, may have thought you were unsuitable to adopt; you may have a serious medical problem and would be unable to care for a child in the long-term; you could have a drug or alcohol problem; and many other reasons…

The door to the holding room opened, and the Chair came in—she gave us the good news that we were approved. I smiled at Jane and we squeezed each other's hand. I felt like a heavy load had been lifted off our shoulders. Now, all we had to do was wait to be matched with a potential child.

The Social workers let us know that there were two brothers that might be suitable for us—but they quickly realised we lived too close to the birth parents, so they offered them to another couple in our Prep Group. This was only mildly disappointing, as it was over quickly.

We decided to celebrate being approved as adopters, by going on holiday.

We were staying in a lovely chocolate box cottage on a farm. Whilst we were there, we got some sad news that Jane's granddad had been rushed to the hospital and was in a coma—he was in his eighty's and had been slowly getting sicker.

That week we also received a call from a social worker. They had a little boy that they thought could be a good match for us. We were so excited!

Part Two: David's Story

When we got back from holiday, we met up with the child's social worker and she briefed us on his background, including medical history. The child's social worker is always a different person to the social worker that helps you through the adoption process. The baby boy was undergoing tests on his physical condition, as the doctors weren't sure whether he had some kind of disability, such as cerebral palsy. Nevertheless, we were so excited to have been chosen, that we 'swept the comments under the mat' and decided we wanted to go ahead.

The baby was supposed to have been taken for the various doctor and medical appointments, but the foster carer kept cancelling them. This delayed the adoption service's Medical Officer from filing a report—this is required before the child can be placed with a potential adopter. They advised us that we would need to wait for the report before we finally decided.

We were so excited that we could have a baby boy soon, so we told our parents and our very close friends. They were pleased for us.

In the meantime, Jane's granddad had died. We went to his funeral. We felt joy about the potential child and deep sadness about Jane's grandfather. It was like our emotions had been put in a blender.

The social worker arranged for us to meet the foster carer and watch the baby playing—she had been looking after him for nearly a year. We weren't allowed to have physical contact with him, but just to act as the foster carer's friend.

The social worker said she couldn't make the meeting, but was happy for us to do it on our own. He was a happy and energetic baby, crawling around the floor. We couldn't see any physical problems, but then again, we weren't doctors.

Later the baby's social worker called to say that the Foster carer complained we'd tried to pick up the baby—which was of course not allowed. That wasn't true. Our social worker believed us after digging a little deeper.

Eventually, we discovered that if you had fostered a child for one year, you would preferentially be considered above all other adopters, to adopt that child. I think her comments in combination with the medical appointment she cancelled, was her way of trying to delay the proceedings to her favour.

Once she reached the end of twelve months, we heard that she'd applied for adoption, and we were forced to withdraw our interest.

We were devastated.

We heard nothing back from the Social workers for many months. One of the other couples in our Prep Group was already matched with a child, and he would be moving in with them soon. Jane and I felt conflicting emotions of being happy for them, and incredibly jealous at the same time.

Part Two: David's Story

In hindsight, the baby boy was probably not the right fit for us. There was the possibility he could turn out to be disabled and be on crutches for life. Or perhaps with some physical therapy, he would be fine? It could have taken years to manifest and we didn't want to wait years to find out.

Our Adoption Adventure

Part Two: David's Story

CHAPTER ELEVEN:

Hope

A year had passed since the Adoption Panel approved us. I was now 40, and Jane was 33 years old. We received a call from a social worker about a girl called Summer that could be a good match for us.

We were really excited! But having been burned the first time around, we tried to temper our excitement a little. We decided not to tell our friends and family, just yet.

A week later we met with Summer's social worker to discuss her background. We were the best match out of three couples they had shortlisted. Her reports looked good. Not only that, but she also had a little brother.

The week after that we met with her Foster carer—we insisted our Social worker attend with us, following our bad experience. The following day, we met Summer for the very first time. She was a cute fourteen-months old girl with blonde hair and blue eyes. She had a playful attitude but was a little shy. She could just about walk and could mutter a few simple words. She was adorable.

We told the Social workers we were excited to go ahead. They sent us a huge number of documents, detailing observations and assessments of the birth parent's ability to look after a child. They were written by Social workers, Doctors, Midwives and other professionals. It was so sad to read about the conditions and care she experienced as a baby. There was example after example of things that had happened, that showed the parents were unfit to look after her. It wasn't Summer's fault—we felt for her.

Four days later we had a Post Adoption Support Planning meeting with our social worker, to see what assistance we might need. We also met with their Medical Officer, who didn't have any concerns about Summer's health or development.

We were given a date to go to Panel again in two weeks time, to decide whether Summer should be 'placed' (live) with us. Things were moving really fast!

The day of Panel came, and we were approved! Yay. I don't remember much about that second time. I think we were more relaxed, and perhaps due to the speed things were going, we hadn't had much time to worry and get stressed.

The month was a whirlwind of activity. Adoption is almost like finding out you're pregnant…then giving birth a month later, as that's how little time you may have before they move in!

I put together a Welcome Book for Summer. It was a talking photo album. I took photos of our house, the local park, our cat, Jane and I and our immediate family. Then I did a voice over for each page. I also photographed a soft toy in some of the photos. They gave the book and the soft toy to the Foster Family, so Summer could get familiar with us.

Meanwhile, we quickly bought toys, a cot, pram, nappy changing kit, nappies, clothes and all the toddler paraphernalia you could imagine. We hadn't done it earlier, as we didn't know what age or gender our child would be.

Two weeks later, we started having regular visits to Summer's foster carer's house, to play with her. Now we were allowed to hold her hand and pick her up. We took her to the nearby park to play. She loved the swings.

A few days after that, the foster carers brought Summer to our home, to help her become familiar with the environment, and our cat River.

After a fortnight we collected Summer and drove her home. That was a really special day for us, and a sad one for Summer's Foster carers, who'd grown very attached to her. I'm sure if they'd been younger, they would have tried to adopt her themselves.

We invited them over a month later, to see how Summer was getting on—they really appreciated it. We stayed in touch with them after Summer moved in, and they sent her Christmas presents for a number of years afterwards.

I have many fond memories of those first weeks with Summer. She could say 'no', 'yes', 'num num' (food), and 'Mama'.

She called me 'mama'. I would tell her 'not the

Mama'—then point to myself and say 'Dada'.

One day we were walking through a shopping mall with Summer. She saw a balloon salesman with a huge floating SpongeBob SquarePants and excitedly walked over to him. She pointed and said "SpongeBob".

"I can't believe she learned to say SpongeBob before Dada", I said to Jane. We bought it for her and tied it to her pram. She spent a lot of time admiring it.

Summer bonded with Jane really quickly—I always became the second choice if Jane was within view. If Summer hurt herself and I went over to help, she would always hold out her arms to Jane instead of me; even if I was the closest to her. It was hard on my emotions being rejected so often.

I talked with some of my male friends about this, and they all told me they'd experienced similar situations. That was reassuring. One of them recommended I did bath time with Summer on my own. That really helped. But even to this day, she's still a mummy's girl.

Summer had trouble sleeping when she was a baby. Unfortunately, I have a really sensitive hearing, so I always got up to see to her at night. Jane carried on sleeping…oblivious to it all. I remember some nights when she cried every half an hour, all night long. I ended up taking a nap during the day when she slept, in order to catch up with my sleep.

Summer's usual wake up time was four in the morning, as one of the foster carers did early shifts. That took a bit of getting used to, but we managed to gradually get her to sleep in until six over a couple of months.

We accidentally discovered that hearing 'Love love" by Take That would send her off to sleep. So I spent many a night listening to that song on repeat, whilst I held her to my chest and gently swayed.

We were finished with the adoption process, or so we thought.

Being 'placed' (living with us) was not a done deal. Social workers visited our house for the next six months to check on Summer and us. It never felt relaxing, being under a microscope. There was also a surprise home visit, which is normal procedure.

It was hard on our family and friends when Summer moved in. Following the advice of the Social workers, we weren't allowed to introduce Summer to anyone for weeks, and when we did, it was months before they were allowed to touch her, or do any care tasks. This was to ensure a solid bond with us. It was difficult for our parents to restrain themselves, as they wanted so much to pick Summer up and hug her.

By now, the other members of our Prep Group were all in various stages of their new children moving in. We regularly chatted with each other but had the tricky situation that we couldn't meet up until our collective children had bonded with their adoptive parents.

Our Adoption Adventure

Part Two: David's Story

CHAPTER TWELVE:

It's a Boy

We were soon contacted by the social worker for Summer's baby brother Christopher and started going through the same introduction process. Again this was a different social worker.

Initially, we visited without Summer, so we could start to build a bond with him. Christopher was less than a year old, so he was mostly crawling and didn't talk. He was obsessed with wheels and would lie with his head on the floor, moving cars back and forth and watching the wheels turn.

Summer liked constant interaction, but Christopher preferred to play on his own and had incredible focus on small actions. He also didn't like loud noises. In hindsight, these were warning signs of his condition.

The Medical Officer had some concerns about the delay in Christopher's development. So we waited for the results of more tests.

At home we'd been showing Summer photos of Christopher, to get her used to his appearance. We finally brought Summer to the Foster carer's house to meet him. She'd never lived with Christopher, so I think she was too young to comprehend that he was her brother. It was just a play date to her.

Six months after Summer moved in, we brought Christopher home. The thing I remember most about that day was seeing Christopher and Summer reclined in their car seats, fast asleep—their heads were tilted towards each other. I took a photo of that special moment. They looked so cute.

We only had two bedrooms, so we placed a cot in our bedroom for Christopher and hung a heavy curtain around it to give us a little privacy. We had to be so quiet going in and out of our room, in order not to wake him.

We had planned to convert our loft space into two additional bedrooms. But the adoption service doesn't like the disruption of building work during adoption, so we decided to postpone until we felt the children would feel secure enough to handle another change to their environment.

Very quickly Summer 'clicked' and realised that Christopher wasn't going back. He would be here forever.

Her behaviour started deteriorating, as she wasn't getting as much attention anymore. She didn't like him to eat with her, so I ended up feeding Christopher in the kitchen. It was lucky I worked from home. I don't know how the couples with husbands working all day would cope—especially as you're not supposed to have anyone help with care tasks for the first few months.

But it bought some blessings. I have many fond

memories of sitting on my bed in the dark feeding Christopher a bottle of milk, then laying him down for a nap in his cot.

If Christopher hurt himself and Jane ran to give him comfort, Summer would scream—not because she was worried about Christopher, but because Jane's attention had focused on Christopher, and she wanted to draw more attention to herself. We didn't realise this for a while, but it persisted when she got older, (and it wasn't exclusive to Christopher).

Our first Christmas as a family was magical. We took so many photos of the day. Afterwards, we went to a professional photographer to take photos of our children, and us as a family. We sent our families photo mugs, and printed canvases. There's a huge one of us on our lounge wall in matching purple t-shirts. I'm so glad we did it whilst they were young. Guests always comment on how lovely the canvas is.

Finally, we attended a court, to legally adopt Summer with our family name. She got a certificate, and we all stood with the judge for a photo.

What a journey so far. It had taken three years from attending the initial presentation on adoption, to actually adopting a child. It had taken a lot longer than we thought it would.

Christopher continued to have appointments with various consultants about his development. He seemed happy, so we weren't overly concerned but hoped he would catch up as he grew older.

We arranged a number of days out with our adoption Prep Group. It was so amazing to see that everyone had a child, including the two single women. Out of the six family units, two of us had more than one child. It was great for the children to spend time with others in the same situation. The grown-ups discussed any parenting issues, and things specific to adoption that our family members just wouldn't understand. We still meet with this group of friends a couple of times a year.

Unfortunately, life wasn't full of hope and happiness for everyone in the Prep Group. One couple thought they were also going to adopt their daughter's sibling—but things dragged on for a year, and eventually, it never happened.

Another couple who'd adopted two boys got divorced. The adoption process is a huge strain on your relationship, so you need to be strong before you commit to this path.

Our social worker put us in touch with an adopter in our town. She arranged some coffee mornings, where we met other local adopters. We made some good friends from that group and set up a number of play dates.

We also met a couple going through the approval process but hadn't been matched with a child yet. They already had a birth child, but couldn't get pregnant again. Their wait was a long one, spanning many years—but eventually, they were blessed with two girls.

Part Two: David's Story

After many more tests and meetings with consultants, Christopher was finally diagnosed with Sensory Integration Disorder (SID), part of the autism spectrum. It affects his senses. He can become *over stimulated* by sounds. If someone used a hand dryer in a toilet, he would hold his hands over his ears and start crying.

He also has difficulty with proprioception. Before meeting Christopher, I'd never heard of proprioception—it's how he can wrongly interpret the position of his body parts and feelings of pressure, which affects balance and the strength of his movements.

Conversely, Christopher has no problem if he is the one making really loud noises. He can imitate police and fire engine noises with his voice that are so loud and realistic, that people look to move out of the way when they hear him.

Equally, sometimes he needed *more stimulation* in order to get himself to the right level. One of the things he liked to do was 'flapping'. He would hop in a bright hallway, with a hard floor. Even if the hall was filled with bright sunlight, he would always turn on a light.

He flicked his ears at the same time as he hopped. He used to make a groaning noise whilst he did this, but now he rarely makes a sound. He doesn't like people watching. He generally only does this at home, and not at other people's houses. Although when we go on holiday, he designates one area as his 'flapping zone.'

He likes to jump on the trampoline and be tickled, as alternative ways of increasing stimulation. If he's sitting still, he needs something to fidget with, in order to stay in one spot for any length of time. This makes it more challenging at school, and meal times.

We had a double swing in our garden, and Summer and Christopher loved being pushed on it. I have a video of my father swinging them, and Summer was saying "wee" every time she swung forward. They never seemed to tire of it. Unfortunately a couple of years later my father died. That movie is one of the few I recorded of him playing with them.

The council's adoption service funded some Theraplay sessions, to give him extra stimulation and build his motor skills. He absolutely loved these and often asked when he could play with 'the lady' and her jungle gym.

I think autism is getting more common, due to an improvement in diagnosing children. Amongst the friends I know well, there are three birth children diagnosed as autistic. These are all parents who didn't drink or take drugs during their pregnancy. It could happen to anyone.

Social Services continued to visit our home for many months, to observe Christopher. We put together a photographic 'Life-story book' for both him and Summer, to remind them of their adoption journey. It showed their favourite toys, food and other things as a baby. It had pictures of our home, Jane and I, our pets, and immediate family. It told the story of:

- Where they were born

- Who their birth parents were
- Why they were removed from their care and put up for adoption
- Their foster carers
- Why we were chosen to be their parents

We felt their Life-story book was really important to help them understand their adoption, so we made time to sit with them once a week as they turned the pages. As time went on, we did it once a month, and now it's every couple of months, or whenever they ask.

Once a year we write to their birth mother and give her an update on Summer and Christopher. She usually writes back. This is done via a social services 'Postbox' to keep our name and address confidential. She split up with her husband and he didn't give social services a forwarding address, so we couldn't write to him.

Eight months after Christopher moved in, we had our celebratory day in court to officially adopt him.

One major advantage of having an adopted child is that you are guaranteed to get into any state school you want—you go to the top of the list. So when it came to selecting an infants school for Christopher, we chose an 'Outstanding' one a mile away, that we wouldn't typically have been eligible for (as we were outside their catchment area). The school helped us to apply for an Education, Health and Care (EHC) Needs Assessment (previously known as a 'Statement'); this has enabled the school to fund a dedicated person to help him improve.

To the outside world, most people wouldn't guess that

Christopher had a condition. He's an energetic extrovert, willing to get stuck into anything. It's only the educational staff at pre-school and then at school that noticed his delay, as he's about a year behind his peers in reading, writing and mathematics.

Christopher has always been a 'ladies man', even as a toddler. When we took him to parties, he'd always find the prettiest woman in the room. He'd try to make her laugh, and then attempt to climb on her lap, so he could have their attention. He'd chat to women in supermarkets, and now at only seven years old, he's started having girlfriends.

Loss of relationship attachments can manifest themselves in different ways. For some, it can make them super-clingy like Summer, who want to protect their relationship with their primary caregiver. For others like Christopher, they have the opposite impact, and they try to charm complete strangers in order to widen their relationship network. We're aware of the situation and monitor it. This doesn't only affect adopted children. It can similarly affect those children whose parents split up or die.

* * *

Three years after attending that first adoption seminar, our family was now complete.
Looking back over our journey, if I'd known everything that was going to happen, would I have adopted?

Absolutely. Although I'd liked to have started much earlier.

Part Three: An Interview With Nanna

CHAPTER THIRTEEN:

What was it like being a parent?

I'd always wanted to be a parent from the time I met Granddad. I was brought up with the expectation to get married and have children. I'd had no experience with babies, as I was the first to have one in my circle of friends and family. My Mum gave me lots of support, as she'd been a registered nanny—but no support from my mother-in-law. I didn't have any other local family at the time. I got pregnant the first month I tried, and I was really happy.

I joined an NCT group and did the training. It was a great resource, and I stayed friends with a couple of the mums for years.

When I had my baby it was a shock to come home with this bundle—but they do survive!

When you turned one year old, we had a birthday party.

Our Adoption Adventure

You fell asleep afterwards, and Granddad and I got around to having sex again. We wanted a few more children, so we thought we'd go for it. Your sister was conceived that day—I didn't think it would happen so quickly! So there is one year and nine months between you and her. I'd been told it was easier to have children closer together, and we'd planned on having four children. It was quite common to have small age gaps between children in those days.

People had told me that if I'd had another baby, you'd calm down a bit. But that didn't work. Neither you nor your sister slept at all—and when you were awake you were whining.

Granddad would look after you, and I'd look after your sister—as she was much more difficult to handle. When your sister turned two, it was so awful that we decided there was no way we were going to have any more—we wanted a good nights sleep.

You started playschool when you were three years old—we had to pay for it, but it was worth every penny. It was nice having two girls close in age as you grew up—you occupied yourselves, playing together. You liked dressing up and playing with dollies—but you did fight as well. There was a lot of "it's not fair."

Things were easier until you became teenagers, and started hating us. You always pushed the boundaries—if I said come home at ten in the evening, you'd be home at quarter past ten. So when your sister turned your age, we didn't do that. We just said, "come home when you're ready." And she'd come home at ten.

It is difficult when you have two children because they both want the same things, and sometimes you can't when one of them is not old enough.

Motherhood was what I'd thought it would be…only harder!

There were some fantastic times…some really wonderful times…but there were also some times where I did wonder why I'd bothered. The amazing times offset the awful times.

Our Adoption Adventure

Part Three: An Interview With Nanna

CHAPTER FOURTEEN:

Your Thoughts on Jane Not Conceiving

Gutting! Absolutely gutting!

I hated even talking about it with you. It was so awful. Every month you said, "No I'm not pregnant...I'll tell you when I'm pregnant." We could see you were getting more and more upset by it because you expected to get pregnant right away.

And then you tried IVF. I still remember that day, when you were around our house and had discovered that the IVF hadn't worked. David was away on business, and you had to walk up the hill to get a signal on your mobile phone and call him with the sad news.

I remember that day so vividly, as you'd been through hell and back with all those injections and operations—and the damage it was doing to your body. Emotionally it was a roller coaster that I wouldn't want to get on myself.

You not getting pregnant via IVF was THE biggest disappointment in my life. I didn't think your sister wanted children at all, so if you couldn't get pregnant, then we were never going to have any grandchildren. You were my only hope.

Had I not had a hysterectomy, maybe I could have been your surrogate? Although my age might have discounted me.

And then there were all your cousins getting pregnant during that time. I didn't want to talk about them with you. Pregnancy should be celebrated, but talking about it would have been like 'kicking you in the teeth' when you were already down.

Part Three: An Interview With Nanna

CHAPTER FIFTEEN:

Then You Told Me You Were Going to Adopt

I remember you had a lot of tasks to do for the adoption process, just to 'tick the boxes,' such as essays on your feelings. It appeared to be a whole day of homework a week, every week, for a year—that was half of your weekends gone.

There was that awful fiasco when you met the baby boy, and the foster parent made things up about you to try to get you thrown out of the adoption process—so she could adopt him instead. That should never have happened.

Meeting Summer and Christopher for the first time aren't vivid events in my mind. I think it was because you told me so much information about them, and I'd seen photographs. Summer was difficult to handle after Christopher turned up—she was too young to understand what having a brother meant.

Due to the guidance from the social workers, we didn't see Summer for a month after she moved in with you—that was quite hard on us. But I respected your wishes, as you'd been indoctrinated on the adoption process by the social workers.

I don't remember much about Summer and Christopher's first Christmas, except for David feeding Christopher a bottle of milk. It was fairly low-key as you had been asked to make it almost like a normal day.

* * *

I think the adoption process was really time-consuming and had a lot of paperwork. There was a lot of soul-searching and tearing your heart to pieces. It almost feels to me as though they break you down…and then they build you back up again to fit the adoptive-parent mould.

The social workers want you to take off your rose-tinted glasses, so you can imagine the worst case for those children going into care…but inside, you still hope you will adopt a 'perfect' child.

My tops tip for other would-be nanas is to lower your expectations. The adoption process will be hard but believe that yes, you will get grandchildren.

Also support your son or daughter, especially when the adoptive child arrives—perhaps clean their house once a week, as I did for you. Be prepared to step in and do as much of the mundane tasks as possible, to free them up to focus on the adoptive child. I remember doing the 'walk of sleep.' Walking the streets for hours with Summer in the pink pram—and the minute we got home she'd wake up again!

Part Four: Our Children's Thoughts

CHAPTER SIXTEEN:

An Interview with Summer–8 Years Old

What is adoption?
Someone takes a child because their other family doesn't look after them properly. They get put into a new family and if they can't find a family straight away, they go into foster care. Then once they get adopted they go into their new family forever.

What do you feel about being adopted?
It's good. Because if I was still in my old family then they will not be able to look after me properly, even if I'm still a child. I don't really worry about it. I don't think about it much. I'm happy to be adopted because otherwise I wouldn't be treated very nicely.

Do you ever talk about it with children who have been adopted like you?
No – not even with adopted children. If I wanted to I

could talk about it, but I don't really at the moment.

What would you say to help a little child who was about to move to their forever family?
To give them advice I would say, be calm, be nice, be respectful and helpful so that their mummy and daddy say "that is a wonderful child". If you are feeling scared don't think about and just do it.

CHAPTER SEVENTEEN:

An interview with Christopher–7 Years Old

Christopher is delayed by one to two years, so he doesn't yet have a full understanding of adoption. He also doesn't remember anything about his birth parents, or foster placement, as he was only ten months old when we met him. With that in mind, here are his responses.

What is adoption?
Hello. I was born into a different family. I don't like talking about it.

How do you feel about it being adopted?
I feel good about being adopted because it feels so right—having a nice family. I really like my Mum because she does the lovely singing.

What would you say to another child who was about to be adopted?
I'll help you. Go to the doctors right now. Because there's going to be a baby coming out!

Our Adoption Adventure

Part Five:

CHAPTER EIGHTEEN:

Conclusion

When we set about writing this book we decided to write our sections without reading the others first—so we could be as honest as possible about our feelings. It has been interesting looking at our experiences from different perspectives. We have learned a few things about each other.

I know what a tough time my parents had, but we only talked about their experiences years after the fact. We were sensitive, and they did what we needed and asked them to, keeping their thoughts to themselves. I am grateful for their support and tolerance!

Summer has a pretty good understanding of her situation and is dealing with it well at the moment. I am sure we will struggle at various points as she gets older, and we are mindful of how it will affect her self-esteem.

Christopher has a less accurate idea of what he has gone through—but he doesn't seem troubled with it at the moment. We will continue to talk with him about adoption, so his understanding will grow over time. He is not a typical seven-year-old. His emotional maturity and understanding of complex concepts are more like that of a five-year-old. We did laugh at his answers though!

So I wanted to finish this book with some thoughts about our overall experience, feelings about the adoption process and advice I could give you…

Part Six:

CHAPTER NINETEEN:

Our Ten Tips for Adopters

1. Prioritise Your Marriage
We call ourselves a "Team Carter". David and I are the founding members; Summer and Christopher complete the team. Our roles as parents are important—but our marriage is key—without it, the team falls apart, and the children would experience more loss.

We were together for fifteen years before we were parents, and will be together once the kids move out and have families of their own. Although we have to prioritise taking care of our kids day-to-day, we have to function as a couple as well.

When we were in the trenches of early parenthood, with a one-year-old and a ten-month-old to learn to look after—we didn't spend enough time together. It might be sustainable for a few years, but not indefinitely. When the kids got older and started pre-school we started to have more time to be a couple, rather than constantly putting our own needs second.

This can be good for couples like us, or bad for others. We know one couple who came out of this phase, then got divorced. Although it is awful—and my heart goes out to them and the children—I can understand it. When you are in the thick of it you're in "emergency mode". Things can be bad, but you ignore it as there is always something else that takes priority. When you start to get your lives back, you find that your marriage is beyond repair. Sometimes the pressure has been so great that we have been right to the edge of a breakdown—which is terrifying.

My advice is to schedule in a "date night" at least once a month. Go out for a meal, go to a spa for the afternoon, have sex—even if you don't feel like it. Apologise for being 'pissy' with each other. Hug. If you don't, then when you get out the other side, there will be no relationship left to save.

Although you want children, and parenthood is important, you will be married and together once they have gone—and that is equally if not more significant.

Apologies to those who are not in a relationship, if this seems irrelevant. In which case, perhaps it is your close friend or family member that is your 'partner.' Assuming that you plan to be in a relationship at some point, hopefully, some of it may be useful. Remember, you're a person as well as a parent.

2. Your Health Is Key
You only get one body, and you can't help your kids if you're sick or dead.

Part Six:

I got this one wrong for a while. David and I let our weight slip in our twenties—so we subsequently made an effort to get back to the normal-ish weight range for IVF and then the adoption medicals.

The first couple of years after placement were extremely full-on for us, so I cherished the chances I could sit down alone with food, such as nap times and bath times. We were not eating particularly well as a family, with pre-packaged meals, chocolate spread sandwiches, pancakes and junk food, for us and the kids. This was partly exhaustion, and partly a mental reward for getting through the day.

I put on nearly three stone. Although I didn't have any health issues, I realised that if I carried on, my health was going to get worse. A couple of things tipped me over—I had a new passport photo taken—and realised my face looked almost round. I ordered a pair of pyjamas online in a 16 and trying them on found they were too tight. I realised I was a food addict.

I made a decision, and with David's help, I lost all the weight and more over the next two years. I've maintained the loss for over three years—and now exercise and healthy eating are a part of my values. Losing weight can be easy—people do it all the time—maintaining a healthy weight is key.

The kids have benefitted from a healthier diet, and are fit and strong themselves. Feeding an autistic child, and a girl who barely wants to eat (unless it's junk), has been a challenge, but we are widening their palates as best we can. They are both extremely healthy—and we are grateful for that.

3. Make an Effort to Have Friends Who Are Adopters
We have a network of people who have adopted children—our boot camp families, and a local group that was set up in our town. You will be surprised how many people have adopted near you—reach out via the school or Facebook. Many people don't tell anyone locally and I think that the children and parents would benefit from chatting to others who are going through experiences similar to theirs—if nothing more than to compare notes and to get hugs and sympathy. Adopting is stressful, and having a good support network of friends and family will help you to cope.

I think the future benefit to the children is enormous. They will have other peers to talk to, who are part of their "club". So they aren't the only weird kids with a complicated history. We're waiting for that to pay off with ours—they haven't really started talking about it with anyone else yet.

Children will have different feelings towards being adopted. We have a good friend who recently adopted two girl siblings (having an older birth child already). Bizarrely they ended up joining Summer's and Christopher's classes in school. Being adopted older (six and seven), the children had a complete understanding of their situation—and talked about it with their teacher and others in their class. My children reacted negatively to this. Summer—who is shy, was happy for the girl to talk about her own adoption publicly. However, Summer didn't want the girl to talk about Summer being adopted in front of the other children, particularly her friends. I can respect that, and my friend's mum had a quiet word with her daughter about mentioning Summer's adoption in class.

Christopher, on the other hand, is younger, and although aged seven, he is more emotionally like a five or six-year-old. He has some sort of understanding about his adoption and often talks about it in a fantasy world way (i.e. when we pass an interesting house—"my birth mum used to live there", "she had a car like that").

The adopted girl who joined Christopher's class is a real sweetie—and again presents as younger than her age. They actually became best buddies with no prompting from the teacher or us, and although Christopher hasn't got a very good understanding of his own history—he found a like-minded soul in her. Now we have moved, we're making an effort to stay in contact with the family, as we all benefit from the time we spend together.

Us adopted parents can support each other and can understand the massive efforts we make to manage our kids through the day sometimes. The children can hang out, and will over time have people they can share their thoughts with; to know they're not alone.

4. Be Open to Talking about Adoption with Your Kids
This was hard at first, as we weren't forced to do it. It was difficult for our kids to avoid, as we had social workers in our house regularly—but they were young, and didn't really have much of an understanding.

Once we had legally adopted our children, and the kids

grew older and their comprehension expanded, we had a period where we didn't really talk about it at all. We designed some really lovely Life Story Books, and brought them out occasionally—but the kids just wanted to look at the pictures of themselves and our family. We got better at mentioning it, as we felt more established as a family, and fortunately now (age seven and eight) we talk about it fairly casually.

When our friends adopted, it brought it to the front of their mind again. The same thing happens when we meet our boot camp families a couple of times a year.

Writing this book has given our children another opportunity to think about their adoption—we bought out their Life Story Books again. As they get older and start to process it in more complexity, we will give them more information, including the detailed reports from social workers and medical staff. They will also have some friends who they can talk to if they don't want to talk to us.

Never keep it a secret from your kids. Because WHEN they find out, they will find it hard to trust you again.

5. Be a Champion

To get through the adoption process you have to be fairly tenacious. There are plenty of times when, if we had been "so-so" on having children, we would have just thrown in the towel and gone and sat on a beach. Being an adoptive parent requires more than this.

Examples are:

- Once we had Christopher placed, the social worker told us we should adopt them both at the same time, once they had decided both children were settled. Being placed many months earlier, it didn't seem fair for Summer to have this uncertainty, so we pushed to get Summer's adoption order first. It made more work for them, but I'm glad we did, as we could relax a little, safe in the knowledge that at least part of our family was legally secure.

- We made the decision to use our rights as a parent of ex-looked after children to get them into the 'Outstanding' school, slightly further away from our house. It was a bit of a faff on the school run—and not everyone understood how we had managed to get them into the school—but it was what was best for our children. I am glad that we did it, and Summer and Christopher thrived in their caring environment. We ended up with amazing teachers, and they went above and beyond to help our kids, and to get Christopher's EHC for him before he left.

6. Be Willing to Learn

Initially, you are programmed on how to be a parent, from your parents. Even if you had bad parenting, you will find yourself reverting back to your default settings in times of stress—it's wired in. The whole adoption process is one of assessment, learning, and breaking your programming.

We must have bought thirty books on adoption,

adopting after infertility, adopters journeys, parenting, psychology, attachment, effects on families, ethnicity, trauma, and so on. Amazon must love us.

We soaked it all up, hoping that we wouldn't need a lot of the "really bad stuff". You have to be willing to learn to parent in a different way—people will tell you that's not how it is done, and look at you oddly; persist anyway. We met someone who really struggled to accept that adopted children needed anything other than basic parenting tools. Fortunately, David and I were willing to try to learn a different way.

We've referred back to a lot of the books, and have learned on the job. We don't always manage to be the parents we imagined we would be, but we do try to do it better next time. We're always learning.

7. Be a Behaviour Detective
Part of the job of parenting a traumatised child (and they all are—even if they are just removed from their birth family), is being a behaviour detective.

When you're getting really angry at your child's behaviour, it can be very difficult to just stop for a second.

I fail all the time, but when I am able to stop and try and get to the bottom of their tantrum/whining/hitting/annoying behaviour, it can make all the difference. I've found that if they have got as far as a tantrum, you just need to wait it out until they move from MAD to SAD. Let them get it out of their system until they are crying rather than screaming, then

Part Six:

you can do something constructive. Talk to them about what is really upsetting them. Take them away from anyone else, cuddle them and get to the root of the problem. This will alleviate the behaviour generally, and you can move on.

There was a really useful analogy that I was taught. We are all like bottles of coke. In the morning you are generally calm, but each annoying thing gives you a little shake. Over the day the pressure builds up—and then it can be the smallest thing, like someone taking a pencil, for your child (or you) to blow your top.

What they are complaining about is probably not the problem—it is that someone was mean at school, or they are scared to go to bed; causing behaviour that seems unrelated.

8. Fill Your Cup

You can't give when you are empty. Like the warning on aeroplanes to put on your own facemask before anyone else's—even your children's. This is a hard lesson to learn and seems contraindicative to a lot that you are taught about parenting.

Yes, your children have needs, and you need to take care of them, but if you are exhausted and have no more patience in you to cope—you are no good to your family. We now schedule in half a day a week—not at the weekend when we have the kids—to do something fun. David and I do this together, so it helps our relationship too, but we have found that if we do not prioritise it we just work all week and parent the rest of the time and have no time to recharge.

If the children have been waking us up all night long, then we go to bed early, or occasionally take a half hour nap.

Fortunately, my parents are great, and our kids stay with them overnight once a month or so—this gives us some special time to work on our relationship and be a couple. We have a meal out, do something we love doing, meet friends, and pick the children up with hugs and full metaphorical "cups". Thanks, Mum and Dad.

Other times when one of us is at the end of our fuse (it happens to the best of us), we are able to leave the house and go for a twenty-minute walk. We are lucky in that we both work from home, so we're able to be a tag team.

All of this relies on having a support network you can lean on, to take the pressure off when you need to. If you are adopting alone, then you need family or friends that you can call on, when you're at the end of your tether. They are quite tough on this during the assessment process (we had to make a pretty chart). We thought listing it out was over the top at the time— but this has proved to be invaluable.

If all else fails, walk out of the room. Make sure your child is not going to stab themselves/roll off the table, and take a deep breath in another room until you are calm.

Find a hobby you can fit into your life that brings you joy, exercise, read a book, make sure you have some

Part Six:

time to recharge, so you can be a better parent.

9. Develop Patience

I'm not a patient person. When David and I do something—we like to get stuck in straight away in. We generally keep hammering away until we get the results we're after.

Unfortunately, although we have the tenacity to keep going, patience is also required when you try to have a baby, wait for specialist appointments, investigations, and IVF on the NHS. The council wanted us to have a certain amount of time between failure of IVF and applying to adopt, attending the first meeting, getting assigned to the training, getting a social worker, and carrying out the adoption assessment. This made the process a lot longer than we'd have liked.

The worst wait was between being approved, to being matched with a child. They were unwilling to tell us when, if ever, that was going to happen. It ended up being a year—but I know people who were matched in one day. Another couple had to go through the courts as they were declined at the adoption panel, and were matched four years later. Most people we knew took less than a year, but the answer seems to be "how long is a piece of string".

All in all, from starting to try for a baby at 27, it took six years for me to have a child at 33. It felt like a lifetime.

Life kind of stops for this period. We didn't feel like we could make any major life changes. Once you're approved, you even debate booking a holiday, in case your number comes up. The way I managed to get through it was by distracting myself with hobbies, reading, and doing the post-approval training, so I could get myself prepared as best I could. Maybe I should have taken up meditation!

We worked with a number of social workers during the adoption process—trainers, our own social worker and various children social workers. They are all kind people, but have a system they are working to—and will always put the children's safety and well being above yours. This sometimes resulted in crushing disappointments, delays and waits that seemed torturous.

One thing that we had to learn was to work with the system, as ultimately, you have no choice. If you want to adopt a child, then you have to do what is necessary to pass their criteria, in their timescale. Although you want to be on the ball and keep things moving—you are ultimately in their hands. We are grateful to our own social worker in particular, who stood up for us when our motives and suitability were questioned. Thank you.

10. Appreciate the Good Times
The past thirteen years—between trying for a baby and now, have been a roller coaster. Talking to our social worker about our relationship, we really struggled to pinpoint anything we argued about at all (they was suspicious that we were lying and we were "too good to be true"). Nope, our relationship was really strong before adoption.

The only issues in our relationship at that point were

the frustration about not being able to get pregnant—
and the resulting goal-driven sex we'd been forced into.
I know from reading other people's stories that this is
pretty common with infertility.

The frustration, grief, fear of failure and microscope
living we endured over the years has required a
herculean effort. Having children and being a mother
was part of my reason for being—a part of my identity.
For those who are on the fence about parenthood, their
relationship could not or would not have endured what
we went through.

The stress of the tests, operations, IVF, grief, the
adoption process itself—and being a parent has taken
its toll on David and I. We've both had periods of
depression. Our marriage has suffered. We've had some
fights where I was not sure whether our marriage would
survive.

Most of this has happened since we adopted and
became parents. Coping with the constant demands of
our traumatised children—managing their emotions and
tantrums has stretched us to the edge and beyond. We
are stable, good parents. We had good enough
parenting ourselves. The anger they can drive us to—
shouting at them, imagining lashing out at them—then
walking out of the room to prevent it from becoming a
reality. Acting in a way that I never thought I would.
Taking it out on each other…

And Then There Are the Positives…
- The excitement of deciding to have a child
- The camaraderie with other potential adopters

- Making it through the Adoption Panel
- Getting a call about a match
- Sharing all of this with our family
- Going out and buying things at Mothercare (for some reason the "baby-on-board" car sign gave me amazing glee)
- Pinching ourselves that we were actually meeting our children for the first time
- The insanity of Introductions—they were actually letting us look after a child on our own!
- First cuddles, smiles, words, teeth, steps, lots of firsts
- Celebrations at court
- Doing it on your own
- Being able to watch your parents enjoy being grandparents
- Being amongst the first on the list at any state-run UK school—guaranteeing you will get in, even if you don't live in the school catchment area
- Feeling complete as a human being

It's hard to see the positives sometimes when you've had a truly horrific day. A really nice day can be spoiled by a tantrum at bedtime.

David and I try to remember to make a gratitude list each day (I have a reminder in my diary otherwise I forget.) Just three things that we appreciate; such as a good cup of coffee, feeling healthy, a sunny day, hugs, having a nice house—whatever. When we are feeling negative my gratitude list can consist of:
The children are alive. I am alive. David is alive.

Part Six:

Be grateful.

In my town, we made friends with one family during the adoption process. We shared a social worker and she often visited us on the same day to save petrol. They were placed before us with a sibling pair, a boy of four and a girl who was one.

We regularly met at Sure Start toddler groups with our kids, and they went to the same school. They didn't tell people that they had adopted, and I think that we were some of the few local people who knew that they had. I respected their wishes, but we were far more open about our situation with friends.

We weren't close but chatted at the gate of the school sometimes. We also helped design some promotional flyers when she launched her business. I didn't see her for a while at school, and her kids were picked up by her husband and extended family. I found out later that she had been diagnosed with terminal cancer and had died six months later.

It could have happened to anyone…even to me. It still could. My heart is heavy for her husband, her children who have already had to endure so much trauma, and have had to be so strong.

Every day with your family is a gift. And you have to start each day fresh if you can. Get enough sleep. Eat properly. Do things that make you feel like an adult rather than just a parent. See friends. Breathe.

So if I knew then what I know now would I do it again?

Yes. I asked David and he said the same.

Is it harder than I thought it would be?

Yes.

Would I rather have just been able to have a couple of birth children and never have experienced the pain that we have gone through?

I am not sure. We are different, stronger people that we would have been otherwise. We are fierce warrior parents who fight for our children. We are "Team Carter." Most people don't know what we have endured so far and will continue to endure behind closed doors, to keep our family functioning in the outside world.

I am fortunate to have good friends, who I can talk honestly with about our experiences as parents. Most of them have birth children. As adoptive parents, we tend to hyper analyse our children, and put a lot of behaviour down to attachment or trauma. My friends seem to have just as much behaviour to deal with—sibling fighting, tantrums, self-esteem issues, autism, etc. My Mum's experiences with my sister and I are a good example. There was no trauma, we were a happy family—and yet we didn't sleep, whined, were jealous and fought constantly. "Normal" kids can sometimes be as much of a handful.

Would we go through it again for another child?

Part Six:

NO! Two is enough, thanks.

Being parents was something that I felt was part of my path in life. I didn't feel like an adult, not having children of my own. I have an amazing relationship with my Mum (despite apparently being a really difficult child to raise). She has been a complete rock for me over the last decade, despite not understanding how I was parenting sometimes. I want relationships like that for myself when the kids are grown up.

Should you adopt?

If that is where you are now—having come to the end of your journey of infertility—or just looking to do so altruistically, where should you go from here?

We set out to write a brutally honest story with all the warts, to help people understand what they were potentially getting into; and also reassure others who are going through the adoption process right now.

Although the training we went through was at times really negative—it only really touched the surface of what it was like going through it yourself. I guess they are treading the line of recruiting more adopters for their children—but at the same time trying to weed out the partially committed, who are likely to crash and burn later. I can't imagine what it would like to be a child in care and have their placement fail. I know a family where this happened—they never went on to have children after that. And we know adopters of children whose first placement failed—this was their second chance. It's damaging to all those involved.

If you "sort of" want kids—or think you should, one of you wants them, your mum wants grandchildren and you think you should oblige—DON'T adopt.

If you feel like having kids is part of your identity—you are passionate about being a mum or a dad, then go ahead. Equally, if you have a birth child and just do not feel your family is complete without another, or feel that you have enough energy in you to love and claim someone else's child as yours—forever—through the worst days and the best—then DO adopt a child.

We've had some amazing times—and continue to do so. We love our children fiercely, we would never go back and change anything. They are affectionate, silly, entertaining, and there are enough remarkable moments to offset the bad, most of the time. We have a purpose and are making our kids lives better every day.

We're still walking down this path, but are far enough along to feel that we have some wisdom to impart to you. We are hopeful that our children will settle down a bit more after our house move. We need to make some new adoption friends in the area. We look forward to helping our children grow up and navigate the choppy waters ahead. Hopefully having grandchildren and helping them cope as parents themselves!

Writing this book has been very hard on our emotions, as we've had to revisit a lot of the sadness in our lives—and I've cried whilst writing. We have both been trying

Part Six:

to get the book written quickly, as it is stirring up a lot of emotions, and we've been mentally drained by the end of each day.

The mood of the court system changes with time. Depending on child tragedy cases, they seem to become stricter or more lenient—making more or less effort to change the birth families behaviour, versus expediency for the children.

We adopted at a time when the criteria for removing children from their birth families was not that strict—things have changed a bit since then, and there seems to be more effort to keep birth families together, even if the conditions and parenting are poor. Friends who went through adoption after we did, reported that there were fewer children coming through the system. No doubt things will change again or have already, that is not something you can control.

Most of all I hope that you've learned a lot more about adoption from the inside. We have shared so much honest information in this book, that we are nervous about letting our friends and family read it. I hope that it helps you with your path.

If you've already adopted and are parenting your kids the best you can—you are not alone. Make some friends who are in the same boat—a lot of us are. Share your stories and give advice when you can.

Most of all—be grateful for your kids, your partner, your family and your life. You only get one (as far as I know), and if you don't stop and appreciate the good things, the moments will pass you by.

Our Ten Tips for Adopters:
1. Prioritise Your Marriage
2. Your Health Is Key
3. Make an Effort to Have Friends Who Are Adopters
4. Be Open to Talking about Adoption with Your Kids
5. Be a Champion
6. Be Willing to Learn
7. Be a Behaviour Detective
8. Fill Your Cup
9. Develop Patience
10. Appreciate the Good Times

Part Seven: Useful Resources

FREE RESOURCES
Visit our website for Free adoption resources:
mycastlepublishing.com/adopt-resources

Adoption UK
adoptionuk.org
We became a member when we started the adoption process. We found the magazine really interesting. But perhaps even more valuable was their local adoption meetings. This allowed us to meet adopters who'd already been through the process and ask them all the silly questions that had been gnawing away at our brains. They also have training courses, which are very helpful.

CoramBAAF
corambaaf.org.uk
Previously known as BAAF. They publish some very useful specialist books, covering topics such as attachment, education, dealing with emotional and behaviour difficulties, and creating life storybooks. We bought quite a few of these.

First4Adoption
first4adoption.org.uk
It contains some great general information on the adoptive process and finding an agency. There's also a useful interactive tool to decide whether you are suitable to adopt a child.

GOV.UK
gov.uk/child-adoption
If you want to know how the system works, this site gives a general overview of the adoption process and criteria.

Printed in Poland
by Amazon Fulfillment
Poland Sp. z o.o., Wrocław